Healthy Children

Only

Need Three Things

Monty C. Ritchings

Book 4 of The Embracing The Blend Series

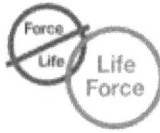

Healthy Children Only Need Three Things

Embracing The Blend, Volume 1

Monty Clayton Ritchings

Published by Monty Clayton Ritchings, 2023.

HEALTHY CHILDREN ONLY NEED THREE THINGS

First edition. August 30, 2023.

Copyright © 2023 Monty Clayton Ritchings.

ISBN: 978-1738875405

Written by Monty Clayton Ritchings.

ISBN 978-1-7388754-0-5

Published by Monty C. Ritchings 2023

Surrey BC Canada

Please check out my website for free tools for change

www.powerfulyoupowerfulme.com

Introduction

Children are undeniably our most important asset, for without them our species will not continue to flourish.

Since we first arrived on this planet, we have borne children, raised them and made more... and yet... we still do not really understand why we have them or what we are supposed to do with them once we have them.

Since time immemorial, we have propagated our species without really understanding even the basics of the whys and whats of bearing these little bundles of joy.

It just seems to be a process we do on default !

Fortunately, our species and society in general have now evolved to the point where we are sophisticated enough and have enough space in our lives to learn the real truth about why we have children and how we can make the best out of the greatest thing we can create in our lives.

The purpose of this book is not to give you rules about how to raise your child to be the best child on the block or how to discipline your child. The purpose of this book is for you to understand the three most important aspects of raising your child that will help you support them in realizing their potential as their most amazing selves.

All human beings are amazing, just in the fact that they have been created. They just need to know it and learn to continually grow with it in the most functional manner.

Although we may not always agree about the fundamental techniques used to raise our children, there are only really three things our kids truly need.

An Important Notice to Our Readers

Disclaimer

My fellow traveler and parent,

I have written this book for the sole purpose of assisting you as a parent, by supplying some tools and information that I feel is pertinent to the process of helping you and your children to gain the most out of your parenting experience.

I am a lay counselor and energetic healing practitioner long schooled in the art of living.

According to those that make up the rules I am not a therapist. It does not matter to me what label is presented to identify me with others. I support all counseling practices that help individuals heal and empower themselves, whether it be in the form of established counseling, energetic healing, yoga, etc. The only thing that matters to me is that you find your own light and express it and pass it on to your children.

With this in mind, I want to make it perfectly clear that this book is not meant to be a substitute for professional psychological help or any other form of intervention that may be deemed valuable or necessary in your healing journey, so you can be the best parent and human being possible.

It is necessary, though, to have you recognize that the lessons procured through working your journey alone are more limiting than along with external support.

I strongly urge you, that as you work through the chapters and lessons in this book that you obtain the support of a person capable of supporting and assisting you in your self-discovery.

This book is intended as a guide for you, not a replacement for the help you may need.

Remember, a candle cannot light itself. My wish for you is that your inner light be illuminated in its own special way, so that it adds to the overall light of all mankind through you, your partner and your children.

Namaste

Monty Clayton Ritchings

May 2022

Index

Chapter 1

Who Are You?

Have you ever stopped to ask yourself this question?

Who are you?

How do you the answer this question?

There are no wrong answers here. You can believe you are whomever you choose to be.

However, there are likely some answers that are better than others. In this chapter, we will start by exploring ourselves and how we perceive ourselves as we live out our lives.

Do you notice these days, no matter where we choose to live, we regularly scc many people who are absolutely obsessed with photographing themselves. You may even be one of them! It does not matter what they are doing, there needs to be a regimen of pictures detailing every step.

The "Selfie" era is well upon us. Click! Click! Click! How many times have you observed people photographing themselves again and again, as they move through their day?

Every time they do something they consider worth noting, there goes another picture. It is a wonder they don't run out of film!

And then they post them on Social Media expecting adoration from their thousands of "friends" who are also Selfie addicts.

Why are these people caught up in this craze?

Another popular craze is "Monday Night Football". These people see their world as an extension of the drama that unfolds as their favorite team marches through the season. These people often find the ups and downs of their life based on how well their team is doing.

So what happens at the end of the season? What happens to the lives of these individuals who see their life expression as a reflection of Monday Night Football?

There are hundreds of other activities that occur in peoples' lives that help them shape who they think they are.

And what about people who are so engrossed in their careers that they know no other way of identifying themselves? Who are they without their job?

So, I ask again, who are you? How do you define yourself?

When we are asked to tell about ourselves and our lives, the normal answer is to paraphrase or sum up the events that have occurred to us as we have lived our adventure.

I am a man, a carpenter, I drive an Audi, I have two children, I go to such and such church and I live in ...

When people identify themselves through photographs, their favorite team on Monday Night Football, their jobs, etc.... they are using external identification.

The truth is that when a person uses outside attributes as their identifier, they are blocking their own ability to know themselves.

The reason for this is that when we ask the question "Who am I?", once an answer is posted, the questioning is usually satisfied, and no other investigation is needed.

Have you ever tried asking yourself a question that you do not know the answer to? Doesn't your mind automatically answer, "I don't know!" I rest my case!

What we need to understand in investigating our answer to the question is... We are not part of the outside world... we are inside this body we carry around with us!

Nothing that one can see identifies who we are, they just tell the story of how we are doing our life. Can you see the difference?

No matter what or who you are, it is likely that this is what an introductory conversation will look like:

"Hi! I am Bob. I live in Langley. I drive a bus. I like to golf. I am married with 6 kids."

Then the other person gets their turn.

"Hi! I am Bjorn. I live in Oslo. I am a fisherman. I have two kids from my first marriage and inherited six more in my second."

After the one person has gone through their list of attributes, and hopefully the other person will get to do so as well and voila! We are on the road to a relationship!

Based on What?

How we develop relationships is often based on how we perceive ourselves and what our emotional needs are at the time of the first interaction... and how we react to the information provided by the other person. Once the glue has dried, the relationship is on. This is usually where politics or something emotionally engaging kicks in, so each individual can test out the commonalities of the other. The more agreements each one has with the other, the more likely they will from a bond.

Then what?

What is the primal purpose of this relationship? How does this relationship fit into your life and what does it do for you or the other person?

There are many people and many types of relationships that flow through the average person's life. Each of them is different and they each serve a different purpose in the overall puzzle that expresses as this individual and their life.

Have you ever stopped to analyze what purpose any of the relationships you personally have, serve in your life?

Most people just accept that these relationships are a part of their life, some here for the long run and some just in the now, without ever stopping to ask what importance this person is for them in their overall life plan. They don't try to find out what this person represents to them.

Why does it matter?

There are a lot of questions that can be asked about the basic operations of our lives and our relationships. If you are a person who seeks to know yourself, you likely have already asked many of these questions. The answering of these continuing questions may take a whole life time... or more. As one question is answered, another question rises.

So, let's get back to the original question. Who are you?

How you answer this question forms the basis for how you structure your life and how well you truly know yourself.

If you believe you are identified through the "things" that exist in your life, then you will likely be a person who chases those things. What is that old adage?

"The one with the most toys at the end wins!"

Life will be a never ending race for collecting things: Homes, cars, trophy spouses, hobby paraphernalia, money and such. There will never be enough.

Some people are actually skilled enough in this game to be able to manage the void they feel through the drive to accumulate stuff, while others will spend their lives chasing a car that goes too fast, leaving them a wreck on the side of the road in life.

Others will choose to avoid the game and live a rather austere life of mediocrity, safe from the gamble that fuels the race. They live in constant dissatisfaction, believing that they were handed the "short straw" in life.

Until people who believe they are what they possess or don't possess, come to a more realistic understanding of how to truly identify themselves, they will likely never find true satisfaction in their lives.

The true answer to the question "who are you?" is not found in the external world. No one can find themselves in their collection of or the avoidance of things.

We are much greater than all the things of the outside world.

The true answer to the question "Who are you?" is:

I am

"I am" is a complete statement on its own.

If you add anything onto this powerful two word statement, you have just created a limitation for yourself.

If today you claim to be a carpenter, but tomorrow you find yourself working as a medical doctor, are you not still the same person?

If you identify yourself by a medical condition, what if you were miraculously cured, do you become somebody else?

Any aspect of how we identify ourselves based on what we perceive in the outer world is a limitation!

We are not our job, our gender, our sexual preference, our ethnicity, our nationality, our body, our religion or any other external aspect we express.

These outer manifestations are just expressions of this particular life we have chosen.

The only correct answer is... I am!

Chapter 2

Hello, Here I am!

Let's start with an exercise!

A couple important notes first:

1. *When you breathe, whether now or anytime, remember to breathe moving your abdominal muscles. This allows your lungs to refresh all of the air in them including at the base of the lungs. If this does not occur, stale air stays in the bottom of the lungs and is redistributed through the blood causing a lack of revitalization (which increases stress).*
2. *Although it is called visualizing you can complete it using whatever sense you like. Most important is that you believe you are actually doing it, and, it is working for you. Use your imagination!*

Seat yourself somewhere comfortable and allow yourself to relax. Sit with your hands unclasped on your lap and your feet relaxed and flat on the floor.

As you settle in, take in three very slow easy deep breaths making sure you allow your abdominal muscles to help.

Now, pretend there is a warm yellow sun beaming down on you from above your head. As you continue to breathe in a very slow deliberate manner, feel the warmth of the sun flowing down into your body.

Feel it flow down into your head, your neck, into your chest, down into your abdomen and down your legs, flowing right down through your feet and into the earth below you.

Take your time and let yourself relax. Remember to keep breathing.

Feel your feet firmly planted on the ground like the roots of a tree. Focus on this feeling for a good moment, then let your consciousness move back up your body through your feet, up your legs into your pelvic region, up into your abdomen, through your chest, into your neck and up to the top of your head and back up to your yellow sun.

Once you have done this action as many times as you desire, allow yourself to relax fully into your chair with no focus but to feel the connection between you and the chair, just letting yourself relax.

Focus on your breaths again and the feeling of being in your body. Let yourself feel every part of your body from head to toe. Allow yourself to enjoy the feeling.

If your mind gets in the way, just stop, relax, focus on taking a deep breath for a moment and let the thought go... and relax.

When you are ready, take a nice deep breath and open your eyes as you exhale.

You have just said hello to your true self!

As we discussed in Chapter 1, you are not all the stuff that follows "I am".

They are just a distraction from the true reality of who you are.

They are only expressions of what you have done with your time or pieces of the package you were given to create your physical appearance.

Now that you have met your true self, please take the time regularly to visit. You have a lot to catch up on!

So why is it important to commune with your inner self?

Once you know the feeling of what you feel like, you can use it to determine what is real and what is not. Your inner voice will have the opportunity, as you practice, to give you messages through feelings that relate to what you do to express yourself as your life moves on.

When we focus on external activities, especially if we are obsessed with them like needing to take selfies a dozen times a day, we avoid creating and maintaining a clear relationship with ourselves. We also find ourselves much more stressed because we lack an anchor to help us base our life on.

When we are able to feel our true selves, we begin to see and understand the facades we have used that prevent us from connecting with ourselves. Memories of many events that have occurred in our lives are held in our subconscious mind that misrepresent who we truly are.

When these events are tied to strong emotions, the binding is just like cement. Issues of abuse and neglect, for example, are strong identifiers that hold us to our past and beliefs that prevent us from expressing in clarity, the amazing person we really are.

Persons who struggle with such strong beliefs may find it challenging to focus on the exercise above. The ego, which has been given the job as our great protector, does not want to let this person go anywhere it is uncomfortable with, so it creates distractions to keep them away.

However, with patience and persistence, and by focusing on the feeling of intentionally relaxing and letting yourself feel good while relaxing, the stranglehold can be gradually released.

The ego is not the enemy in this process; it is just doing its job. It just needs to be retrained! It has been running the show for a very long time on what is likely incorrect information it learned when you were a child.

One of the ego's jobs is to keep us safe. It does this by collecting memories that have shaped our personal perception of our lives.

It then very quickly analyzes current events to determine if they might feel similar to any of those past events and sets up protective devices to "stop the pain" of remembering when necessary.

This can cause a great deal of discomfort for the person in the present tense, especially for those who have suffered dearly at the hands of others, because they cannot see the world around them beyond the memories. They just keep reliving new events as reflections of old, while reliving the pain.

The key point in doing this exercise is to not allow yourself to get involved with thoughts that come up. Just recognize the memory is only a thought, and let it go by focusing on the energy of the sun flowing into you, and your breathing. Eventually, the thought will evaporate, and you can carry on without it.

If necessary you can try journaling on the thought if it is a really insistent one, but be very cautious that you do not reinforce the thought. The goal is to relax and let yourself be who you truly are!

Once you get really good at it, you will be able to dismiss the thoughts quickly and return your focus to the good feeling.

This process does not change your past, but it will certainly change your present and future, as the ego will eventually accept your new program when it realizes the old method of protection does not serve you anymore.

Please understand that this process is not a replacement for counselling. If there are past issues that are still clouding your freedom of expression, please get help. If anything, this process will assist you in your healing and help you change your life.

Be sure to inform your counselor about this work you are doing through the information provided in this booklet, so they can help you more in making changes while utilizing this process.

Once you gain some proficiency in this process, you will realize that you are not your thoughts, or your past memories and you will no longer need to feel that you have to hang onto them. You will have begun your true healing journey.

It is also important to realize that every person on this planet has some memories that cause them to have a tainted perception of their true possibilities.

We are not the only ones who have suffered. In this, it is always best to realize that we are all works in progress and need to be handled carefully and respectfully, especially as we begin to reveal new thoughts, and come to experiences our true selves.

Chapter 3

Karma

Did you know there is more to life than you can actually see?

Many people have a hard time understanding and accepting this statement. I think this is because there is a certain kind of safety in being able to actually use only one's physical senses to determine if something is real.

Fortunately, whether one believes it or not there is an invisible side to life. The great thing about this side of us is that it operates whether we choose to give it recognition or not.

Have you ever thought about what attracted you to a person like your mate or some other person who you just had to know and maybe be with?

That attraction is caused by your invisible side reacting to their invisible side.

I am only going to touch on this subject briefly in this book. If you really want to get into it, please check out my book "**Chakras Demystified**".

The most important aspect I want to share with you is that we do have both an invisible self and a visible self.

Inside the visible self, there are drives that help us to choose situations and people that we either need to attract into our lives or we need to help create, so they can fulfill their (and possibly our) life plan. These belong to the invisible self.

In order to properly help create these bundles of joy according to their long-term needs, they need to choose the right parents in the right situation. This is the beginning of the story; we call Karma and... dare I say... it begins a while before birth.

For example, I recall a dream I had when my wife was pregnant with our son. We had decided his first and second name but could not decide which order. In the dream, I saw my son climb up the outside of our house into our second story window and announce to me the order of his names, then he popped out the window and was gone.

We named him exactly as he instructed!

We are not going to go all Ayurvedic or Hindu or anything here, when explaining this understanding, even though the origins of the word "Karma" are found in these systems.

Very simply Karma is a system of cause and effect.

There are many layers to Karma though. It is not just a thing that happens when you do something bad. It is way more complex than that, but I will try to keep it fairly simple.

The karma we most readily recognize is Personal Karma. Some people are continually conscious of doing things right or wrong because they don't want to create Karma.

The reality is we are constantly creating Karma, because we live in a world of cause and effect.

When we tie up our shoes correctly, we don't fall down. Good Karma... Shoe lace comes undone, and we trip on it and fall, bad Karma.

There are two layers of Karma that are important to focus on at this time because the focus of this book is about our children, so be careful tying up your shoes and let's have a look at them.

Without getting too metaphysical, we need to look at and understand why children are born into the families they find themselves in. The two kinds of Karma are:

- **Personal Karma** that is related to why this particular person has chosen to be born into this family at this time.
- **Family Karma** that is related to the overall spiritual development and history of the entire family, actually families because, hopefully the parents are not genetically related.

If you are interested in knowing more about "soul families" Gary Zukav wrote an excellent book called **Seat of The Soul**.

Personal Karma.

Every person, whether they accept it or not is born to mature as an individual on many levels. These levels include physical, mental, emotional and spiritual and maybe some others.

Over the phases of our lives, we will instinctively focus on one of the levels more than the others as dictated by the very nature of our own inner drives, until it is either satisfied or one of the other levels requires moving into the spotlight.

At the time of birth, when the soul has entered the body for this journey, there is a soft spot or opening at the top of the head. This is caused by the two parts of the skull being separated in order to allow the baby's head to fit through the birthing canal. In time, this soft spot will be closed through the maturation of the bone structure of the skull.

During the time the soft spot exists, the individual is downloading important information from the Universe that will help them to be able to express the life they have now embarked up. This information is stored in the mind but managed by the Pituitary Gland, the Master Gland for our entire being.

During this downloading process, this individual will also learn many lessons from the environment they are living in that will also assist in forming their understanding of how to operate during this lifetime.

This information is gained by observing and participating in the life they are playing in with their family and other people who visit in their life. This information is stored in the subconscious mind and is managed by the ego then reported to the pituitary.

Good or bad, the guidelines are now being created and stored that will define how this individual sees and reacts to the world around them. This process generally continues until the child is around seven years of age.

With the combination of downloaded information from the Universe and that from their local environment, this person now sets out to discover their world and why they are here, while looking through the filters they now carry.

Through the information that has been supplied to them, this person has also attained the foundation of their own karma, the obstacle course that will underlie their "raison d'etre" or reason to be in this life.

Family Karma

We all come from a long line of ancestors who have done lifetimes of learning and activities over the thousands of years we humans have existed. It does not matter what these lessons or activities were, we carry the essence of this learning through our genes and our Family Karma.

When we look back at our family history we can see trends regarding our various levels of expression including our looks, our intelligence, how we handle certain situations, even careers.

If you have had a chance to explore your family genealogy, you will find some really interesting things about yourself, especially aspects that are similar to any of your ancestors.

There is a really interesting debate going on currently amongst scientists and psychologists regarding nature versus nurture. Personally, I do not see it as a debate but as two forms of acquiring information and the tools we need to do this life in order to attempt to fulfill our personal life purpose.

The nature aspect related to information acquired through our genes and thus being family karma while nurture is information acquired while learning the ropes of staying alive in the present.

If I ever doubted the importance of the nature aspect of acquiring information, it sure got proven to me recently.

I grew up in a family of four children plus two from a second marriage. It was easy to tell that all six of us were related, although the two youngers had distinct differences. Recently, through these amazing DNA search programs that are now available, I have a new sister!

She is 5 years older than me, but about the same age as my oldest brother. (My daddy was naughty). The day we met changed our worlds. As I walked into the café to meet her, a massive shift occurred as the world stared at a new set of twins!

Trish and I are so similar in personalities, life experiences, and motivations for living and spiritual beliefs. We look and act more like siblings than my other siblings do to me!

I have since introduced her to some of our cousins. Trish now has a twin cousin as well. They even both have the same kinky hair! Every morning Trish looks in the mirror and says good morning to our cousin Colleen!

It is interesting learning about Family Karma as this new relationship unfolds. Our father provided a great deal of learning opportunities for all of his children through his inability to communicate in an effective and positive manner. His ongoing choices to create learning through physical, mental and sexual violence left the four of us original siblings with a lot of fodder to work through.

What is most amazing is that although Trish was raised by a step father who truly loved her and treated her reasonably well, she chose to marry a man who supported her need to endure the same lessons as our father provided for the rest of us, which she missed through growing up elsewhere.

Family Karma!

Understanding our own Karma is essential to creating wellness and evolution in our own lives. It is by understanding the common and prevalent themes that occur or have occurred in our lives and of our predecessors, that we become aware of what we need to learn through these situations and bring forward into our lives in a positive manner.

Rather than looking at these situations from a victim perspective (if the lesson is considered bad) we can move away from the emotion and peel back the trauma to unveil an opportunity to grow as a human spirit, by turning it into a positive.

No matter the situation, whether yours or any ancestors, no matter how bad, can be reframed into a positive, by changing the perspective and by understanding what was going on at the time.

One key point to remember in this process is that you are looking at an event from another time through your today eyes. You cannot possibly judge the person for what they did, you can only try to understand and draw a positive from what you can glean.

Be sure to keep yourself out of any emotional traps. If you find someone from your past appears to have committed something not acceptable to you, you are not obligated to take on responsibility or guilt for it. Just make sure you choose a better way to express and satisfy the need this person couldn't, if it is deemed part of your path. Only you know for sure.

When we look at the aspect of nurture, it tells us about the methods we have incorporated into our life expression in order to survive and hopefully thrive in this life. As we interact with our environment, we develop rules about survival.

The more emotionally dramatic the childhood learning opportunities, the more nurture has to develop rules in order to cope and survive. This is the basis for personal Karma, at least on the mundane level.

The experience of developing personal karma is different for each child in a family as well, since there are external factors that make each person's experiences different. Pecking order is often one of the most important of these, along with gender as well as what was going on with Mom and Dad during their particular formative time.

If you are interested in learning more about the nurture side, I have written a book called **"Embracing The Blend: What Mom and Dad Didn't Know They Were Teaching You"**.

This book explains two really important aspects for getting through this life alive:

- Understanding and owning your true personal safety
- Understanding and working with your own belief systems

The most important piece of information I can give you regarding Karma is that it is just a starting point and a guide to your own personal evolution for this life time. Karma is not concrete. It is not written in stone! It is written in every moment in your life!

We each have the ability to work with and through our Karma in our own individual way. We are never obligated to suffer needlessly. That is not how Karma works; however, as we live our lives we will make lots of mistakes.

How we choose to deal with these mistakes tells us how we create our Karma.

It is also imperative to understand as we explore our family karma, that we only look at it as an indicator of trends. No person is obligated to follow the family program, however, being aware of such creates the condition where you are aware of the trend, so hopefully, you can do what is necessary to take a different route if it is something you do not want to experience.

A prime example of this situation is diseases. Dr. Bruce Lipton author of The Power of Beliefs is a leading researcher into DNA. His findings state that, just because your family has a propensity for a particular disease, you are not obligated to accept the suffering yourself. Knowing about your family health situations will provide you with tools to ensure optimal health.

Understanding the relationship of beliefs to diseases is a great way to prevent diseases that appear to be common in the family. Louise Hay is a world class leader in this particular field. Her book **You Can Heal Your Life** is essential reading.

Another consideration, especially in regard to health issues but not exclusively, is the location where you or your ancestors spent their lives. Many geographical locations are cesspools for certain diseases, however, your ancestors may not have understood the relationship, so did not know better to leave... I hope you do!

As an example, one is more likely to suffer from the effects of malaria by living in the tropics than by living in the Arctic.

Every person, no matter who they are or what happened to them in their life has free dominion to determine how their life will evolve. It is by understanding the various levels of Karma, along with understanding of the choices they personally make or have made that form the basis of their personal expression, that Karma can be reshaped.

It is the choice of being a victim or a victor in life.

Through making healthy choices based in awareness, one can move away from a destructive life style pattern into something safer and more meaningful that supports healthier growth opportunities for themselves and the people they influence.

No one is ever obligated to fulfill any thought or impulse they have. We all have free choice and a wonderful conscience to guide us!

Not only do the choices we each make affect the outcome of our own lives, but they also support the energy of change for others.

I am not a Bible person; however, there is much food for thought in this book. Exodus 34:7, explains the "Generational Curse". It says that it takes three generations to eliminate the "Sins of The Fathers" (or mothers).

By choosing to recognize choices made by others, and then consciously making different choices, we give traction to the change process.

This was a decision I made when I became a dad many years ago. My grandchildren are safe because the change I chose to implement so many years ago is working.

I cannot suggest strongly enough, the importance of recognizing the events that shaped your childhood as being learning events rather than reasons to empower victim energy.

If you look at them as lessons, you can then make choices that will foster healthier children for you and your spouse.

Remember, all people are born good. Bad is learned!

Chapter 4

Adult Relationships

I want to separate adult relationships from overall relationships. The focus here is the creation and operating of intimate relationships. Relationships with children, since that is the focus of this book will be discussed separately.

In keeping with the discussion in chapter 1, let's continue asking questions and see if we can get to some reasonable and workable answers.

So, let's start off by asking:

Why do we have relationships? Or more accurately, why do we want to have relationships? How do they relate to the original question "Who are you?"

Wouldn't it be easier if we did not bother interacting with other people and just go off and do our own stuff by ourselves?

As human beings, we have had other people in our lives right from the moment we were born (Actually since we were conceived!). We have had people in our lives right through our childhood and right into our lives today. We have learned to incorporate relationships as a habitual part of how we know life.

We have learned through the process of living our life that having other humans around makes life more tolerable and enjoyable (not there is anything wrong with being alone).

There is a much larger reason for interacting and sharing with other humans as well. It is how we learn and how we grow. Without sharing with others in our lives, we become excessively self-absorbed and therefore limited in our ability to expand our capacity to embrace the larger possibilities of life.

Almost everything we know, we learned through the process of nurturing; learning from our environment and other people. It is also the sharing process that drives people to create and to make life better.

Without having other people to share with, would make the creative process almost pointless, wouldn't it!

On a one to one level or intimate level we create and maintain relationships for more selfish reasons. We want to have our wants, needs and desires met at a much deeper level. Many of these aspects can only be satisfied by interacting with one other person (at least at a time).

An aspect of being alive is that we are a living bundle of energy.

Everything that exists is composed of various frequencies of energy. As human beings, we are composed of many levels of energy that combine together to manifest as life and in our case, conscious life.

As mentioned before, my book **Chakras Demystified**, explains our energetic relationships, so I will not go into too much detail here about the energy side of life, but I do want to share some information about the energy of relationships.

We are very fluid energetically. We absorb energy and we transmit energy constantly throughout our lives.

Part of this process is how we communicate. Speaking and hearing are based on receiving and transmitting energy that our mind can process into thoughts. We can then translate these thoughts into action, if we choose.

We also receive and transmit energy through our other senses including touch, taste and smell. What is often missed in the understanding of this concept though, is that we process energy both physically and non-physically.

In the physical world, we like to communicate using our five senses. However, there is more communication that occurs on the non-physical side that provides much more information than we process physically.

Without the non-physical attributes, life would be very robotic.

Like everything else that exists, we are part of the universe as a whole. Everything we do feeds the universal flow. We draw from the universe and we give to it by the very nature of our design.

Somewhere along the line we humans, seem to have forgotten that we are directly fed by Universal Source. In its place we have opted to believe that we can only get the energy we need from other people, or maybe our pets.

We have come to rely on using our five senses in interacting with others to attempt to satisfy refueling our energy.

So what does this do to our relationships?

Until we learn to understand and operate our relationships from a more holistic perspective where we include accessing energy from Source, relationships become a battle ground for controlling the energy that flows between two individuals. The more intimate the relationship, the more energies exchanged and the more tug-of-warring that goes on.

How many times have you experienced the ecstasy of a new relationship where there is an absolute free for all of energy flowing?

So what happens after the honeymoon stage is over?

Right! The fight is on! Whoever can dominate gets the energy and the other suffers until finally the relationship dies.

It does not have to be that way though. Relationships do not have to be a no win struggle!

All we have to do is realize and accept that the energy we crave is ours already. We just have to consciously reconnect with our Source, the Universal Flow of which everything exists.

By reconnecting with Source, we access and absorb the energy we need on our own. This allows us to develop and maintain relationships with others without having to fill a desperate need for an energy fix.

There is no need for a struggle. The relationship then can get on with a more functional focus that is far more satisfying.

So how does one reconnect themselves with Universal Source?

The exercise that is included at the introduction of Chapter 2 is a good place to start. If you do the exercise regularly, you will start to relax more into your body, therefore allowing yourself to feel your true self beyond you external senses.

The next step while doing this exercise is to expand the feeling of being in your body outward beyond the confines of your body.

At first, you can explore the range of your own aura or energy field which normally vibrates out to about 4 feet beyond your physical body.

Once you can feel your aura to some degree, invite another person to join you as you do the exercise. Once you are at the point where you both can feel your own energy field, let your consciousness expand further to see if you can feel the interaction between both of your fields. It will feel sort of like a magnetic pull.

Enjoy this feeling for as long as you wish. It is important to realize that there is no competition in this interaction. You both get to enjoy the feeling equally. This is how relationships are meant to be.

Another fun exercise to try with this is for one person to imagine their aura being really strong and radiant, then to have the other person place their hands in their energy field to try to feel the energy. Eventually, you may even be able to determine which Chakras you are most connected with and which you are not. (These are determiners to what kind of relationship you have currently.)

A final exercise in this matter, is by having both focusing on their energy the holding the palms of their hands toward each other about 4 inches apart will usually let them feel the energy being projected as well.

When we learn to work in relationships in the healthiest way, we will know that our energetic requirements are supplied adequately just because we are designed that way, so, therefore, we can give and receive energy freely with others without fear of running out.

Learning and applying this allows and supports free communication, and keeps us out of the war zone.

When we are comfortable with feeling our own energy field and feeling energetic interactions with others, we can teach our children to do the same thing.

Once we learn to be comfortable with accessing and maintaining our own energy levels through source, it will be more comfortable to let down our guard. After all, isn't our personal energy supply what we are guarding when we pull into ourselves in fear?

Once we are comfortable with this shift, the next step is to learn to observe or witness ourselves. (We actually are quite entertaining!), By observing how we do our life, we become more aware of our strengths and our challenges. Now that we are aware, we can start doing something about them without feeling like our safety is threatened. After all what you are observing are just results of your belief systems.

When we live in our lives in a way that supports our own innate ability to witness ourselves and how we do our lives, we are ready to truly grow in ourselves and make our own life and the world a better place.

Passing this ability and perspective on to our children is the reason we are chatting! After all, the better you function in your life, the better your children will function!

Chapter 5

Recognizing Our Own Belief Systems

Once we are comfortable with feeling what it is like to actually be in our own bodies we now have a good opportunity to work with ourselves and reframe beliefs that are not working for us.

At this point, I choose to reiterate that I have no desire to tell you what is right or wrong when it comes to beliefs. My only desire, is to provide you with information and some tools that will help you to recognize your own belief systems which will allow you to decide whether they are keepers or not.

I also extend an invitation to you at this point to find yourself some support people to help you move through your stuff. Dealing with belief systems is not something you want to do on your own if you are not experienced in it.

It is not that you are likely to hurt yourself; it is just that you will find it more difficult and more tedious doing it by yourself. At some point, it will likely feel like a big struggle and the tendency to give up will strike, so find yourself a counselor or a support group to help you keep yourself on track!

I have mentioned before my book, **Embracing The Blend**. It has plenty of useful information and tools that will help you understand about belief systems and about true personal safety.

A note about true personal safety before we move on.

The exercises we have been practicing in this book help you to take yourself to true safety, for the only place you can access true safety is inside yourself, in the manner described. This exercise is not a form of withdrawal or coping. This exercise teaches you how to reconnect with the true safety that is an innate part of your being.

In order to truly be safe, you must believe you are safe because what you believe in your mind determines how safe you feel.

You can do these exercises till the cows come home, but if you do not believe you are safe, you are not.

Using the mantra:

I am safe and protected,

Doing the exercises will help you move into true safety as it helps you focus on being safe. Keep repeating it in groups of threes as often as you need in order to get your mind to believe it and accept it. Be careful not to allow yourself to become obsessive about it, though, as you may be coming from fear rather than encouraging personal strength.

For the purposes of this chapter, the tool we will use for moving past dysfunctional beliefs is similar to the Sun Visualization we have been using. Other exercises you will find useful are available in my book **Stamp Out Stress** and on **my website.**

www.powerfulyoupowerfulme.com

In order to be able to reduce the effect of beliefs and/or undesirable thoughts, you can use the Sun Visualization with an added component. However, before we add this in, we need to understand how thoughts keep you distracted.

First of all, it is essential to understand that you are not your thoughts or emotions.

Remember, we chatted about this in Chapter 1 when we were discussing "Who Are You?"

Thoughts and emotions are what we call temporal. They belong to the outside world and are not part of you. They are not even friends. They are just things. In that, we have the choice about what we do with the thoughts and emotions that play around in our head.

I want to be clear at this point that I am not discounting the importance of thoughts or emotions. They have their place... and they need to stay there. It is not their job to run your life.

So, let's go to the exercise.

Get yourself settled in and take yourself into your quiet place. Once you feel yourself comfortably relaxed and in your body, let yourself feel what is going on inside of you.

Look at the thoughts and feeling you have going on without interacting with them.

The next step is to visualize your sun in the sky again with its rays beaming down on you. Imagine letting those rays melt the thoughts and emotion in your mind until they fade away. It is just like an ice cream cone melting in the summer sun.

As you do this process, continually take comfortable deep breaths, hold it for a bit, and as you slowly exhale, let the thoughts and emotions lose their power and fade away.

Once your mind is quiet and you have relaxed, focus again on your sun and let it fill you up with warm peaceful recharging energy.

Allow the feeling to stay with you as you open your eyes and carry on with your day.

Any time you are feeling caught up in your emotions or thoughts and choose to shift away, this is a great tool to make it happen. The shift can be almost instantaneous if you let it.

Remember, you cannot focus on two things at once, so if you are focusing on your breathing or the feeling of the warm sun on your body, you cannot focus on the thoughts.

Now let's look at belief systems.

The easiest way to recognize belief systems is to listen to your conversations. Any statements that start with "I" are likely belief systems. This is the time to put on your analyst hat and start paying attention to what you are saying.

Remember, you are the only person who gets to listen to your own rhetoric 24/7!

If you find that you are telling yourself the same statement over and over, it might be time to start looking at that statement to determine if it is a good statement for you to be telling yourself.

You might try keeping a journal logging all the statements you are making to yourself. Pay attention as well to what verb follows "I". I believe. I am. I feel.

Of all the verbs in this situation, "I am" requires the most caution for you because it means you are identifying with this statement as part of who you are.

Try to start, at the beginning of this journey to replace "I am" with something like "I feel". At least then you are just expressing a feeling instead of identifying with the statement.

If you have decided to join a support group or to work with a counselor, having a list of your common statements will help for directing your reframing process. In the meantime, please try to make sure that any statements are supportive and positive.

The goal here is not to rid yourself of beliefs because that would be impossible. The goal is to create a healthy belief system that promotes good health on any level and a good living environment, not just for you but for everyone who is part of your life.

This process is a lifelong practice, so be patient with yourself. Trying to push yourself too hard will only manifest in failure!

One step at a time makes winners! And remember to breathe!

Chapter 6

You and Your Children

Why is it so important to understand about our relationships and about belief systems?

Aren't kids separate individuals from us?

These questions are the key to this whole discussion!

> **Your children are an extension of you and your energies and your karma.**

The comingling of the energies of the two individuals who created this little person did more than just create a body and a new person. With this creation comes a union of the energies that each involved person carries with them.

The child in this situation becomes a joining of the karma of both individuals who participated in the creation. This means that not only did they get your fabulous looks and intelligence; they also get their life purpose through the intermixing of your life purposes. **The Celestine Prophecy** is a great book about this subject by Norman Redfield.

Every person has a life purpose.

It is only by exploring one's own inner drives that allow a person to gain an inkling of what their purpose is. Studying your family genealogy will also help because, if you can get enough information about your ancestors, it will provide clues through their activities about what your purpose is.

Another way that helps determine what your life is likely about is to watch your siblings.

Each of your siblings represents an aspect of your family karma. Watch how they deal with situations in comparison to your own method so you can get a better understanding what you are up to. Learn through their choices and experiences and save yourself the challenge of figuring it out on your own. Again it is about observing your world around you in order to understand who you are and why you are here.

As you observe others, let yourself check how you feel during this period and monitor the thoughts you have. They are key clues to finding your life purpose.

Your life purpose may not be a career move or any other outward expression. It might just be a need to recognize many shifts over your life that need to be made in order to maximize your self-expression and your feelings of self-empowerment.

Why do I care about all this?

The very fact that you are this far in reading this book should tell you something about the answer to this question! This is not a book you would read just before going to bed, so you are definitely in questioning mode.

Being that you are this far into this book, it should be safe to assume that you are a person who is questioning your life and looking for answers about why you are here.

For me, this has been a lifelong quest. Part of my karma is to write and publish these books to help you and others to understand and maximize your experience on this planet. Ask questions... and let the answers arrive!

Do you have any idea what your life purpose is?

Deep down inside you know that your highest purpose is to gain maximum personal and spiritual growth, not only for yourself and your partner but for your children as well... and every other person you interact with.

Now all you have to do is figure out what that path is.

We all love our children very deeply. The information in this book will assist you in being the great parent you desire to be. Through having a good idea of what your life is about, as well as your partner's, you can help your children to find and express their purpose.

The best way to help your children through this process is the answer to the question that caused you to pick up this book to start with.

What are The Three Things Healthy Children Need?

It is finally time to have a look at these three aspects!

Chapter 7

The First Need

Let's have a good look at each of these needs separately, so we can focus on each one individually.

We have already been discussing the first need since the beginning of our discussion in this book.

Healthy Children Need Parents Who Are Aware of Themselves and Growing as People.

Children model themselves after their parents and key caregivers. Children are like insatiable sponges when it comes to learning. Children will learn regardless of the situation they are born into.

The concern for parents should be about what kind of situation the child is being born into, because this will be a deciding factor in what they learn... and how they will deal with life.

I am going to insert a cautionary statement at this juncture.

There is no such thing as a perfect person, parent or situation. The purpose of this book is only to inspire and support you, the reader, to be the best person you can be. We will leave the perfect person, parent and situation to the folks who live in that illusion.

The best we can do is the best we can do... at the time. We could have all done better when we look back; however, life isn't about looking back. Life is about being present now, as we travel through our lives.

As we live our lives, we become aware of situations where we really excel. We also become aware of situations where we really suck... and everything in between. A person who chooses to be aware and proactive in building a good life accepts each awareness as a witness and makes the necessary adjustments as they can and choose.

Besides, who is in charge of determining what is acceptable and what is not?

It is up to each individual to make their own decisions. In making these decisions though, as a parent and as a partner in an intimate relationship, it is important to include your spouse in the discussion (once you have clarity about your situation).

The next step is to determine what effect the choice to be made has on each individual impacted, especially the children. No time for egos here!

Let's have an example.

Mom used to be a smoker. She remembers how she used to enjoy puffing on her cigarettes. Mom decides that she wants to start smoking again, so she goes to the store to buy a pack. On the way, she recalls the agreement she has with her family that any big decisions are to be discussed before going ahead, so she decides to wait on the purchase.

When her family is home in the evening, she broaches the subject with her family.

Immediately tension fills the air. Dad says he does not like the second hand smoke, and he does not like kissing an ashtray. The kids echo his sentiments. Besides mom would have to smoke outside, so she will not be as available to interact with the kids during that time, and they don't like how she would smell when she came back in.

Mom takes all this in, and takes some time to digest what they have told her. She then realizes that the reason she liked to smoke was because it made her feel like she was part of the gang who used to hang out together to smoke.

Her real desire was to be acceptable and accepted.

Mom also realized the health risks involved in taking up smoking again, not only for herself but also her family, so it did not take her long to realize the choice she will make.

She realized that she needed to work on her resistance to feeling accepted, especially important since she now realized she did not need to smoke in order to be accepted in her most important gang... her family.

What kind of decision does dad need to make in his life? Well dad wants to buy a boat and go fishing, so he calls the family together to discussion his wishes.

The kids love the idea, except that dad wasn't thinking about taking them with him all the time. Mom is nervous about the idea because it is a big expense. However, everyone puts their emotions aside and agrees to discuss the matter.

The final agreement that wins everyone's support, including dad's, is that the family will join the local hunting and fishing club, so they can each enjoy participating in nature sports with others. Dad gets to go fishing with his new buddies sometimes because he does need "guy time" while mom enjoys making new friends at the club while not spending thousands of dollars unnecessarily... and the kids learn to enjoy some great outdoor sports. Everybody wins!

When the parents are aware of their wishes and are inclusive of their family in the decision making process, the opportunity for each member to grow increases.. not to mention the bonding that occurs!

And this opens up the conversation to the second need!

Chapter 8

The Second Need

In my first book, **Embracing The Blend**, I spend a great deal of time discussing this very subject.

Safety

Healthy kids need to not only feel safe, but they also need to have a safe environment in order to flourish.

So what is a safe environment?

In my childhood, staying out of the way was safe. My father had a real tendency to use his hands as his primary form of communication. I spent the bulk of my childhood in my bedroom. My older brother, on the other hand spent much of his youth in jail for exactly the same reason.

So, what is safety?

I call it true safety in order to distinguish it from other methods of so-called being safe.

True safety is innate. You are born with it. The slogan of my Embracing The Blend book is:

We are born into safety... Then trained out of it... Now it is time to return!

True safety is the process of creating and maintaining an ongoing environment where anyone who participates in that space can relax and take comfort in being themselves without having to be constantly aware of any issues where they might need to protect themselves or others.

This environment not only allows the participants to feel safe but to be able to (within reasonable guidelines) experiment with life in order to grow as a person.

Pretty well anything outside of this definition would be called "protective safety" or "coping".

As human beings, we are very capable of creating safe environments for ourselves and for others without having to resort to protective practices or coping strategies like medications or hiding in the bedroom.

Healthy children come equipped with the ability to fit in. What they do not have is the ability at younger ages to determine whether their "fitting in" tactics are truly safe or acceptable. It is up to the parents to guide and train them in these matters.

What do children want from their family?

I feel that I need to say at this time that "love" is not the answer. We all want love; however, the truth is that love is an innate part of who we are. We always have love; it is just a matter of how the love is expressed that causes concern.

Whatever we experience as children that gives us the attention we desire is what we know as love… until we learn differently.

A wonderful book on this very subject is **I'm Okay, You're Okay**. It discusses a psychological process called Transactional Analysis. The key point in this book is that children will get the attention they desire. The question is will they get it through positive attention or through discounted attention by acting out.

According to the author, Thomas Anthony Harris, children will derive that attention from acting out even though it takes many times as much effort as positive attention, just because that is what they perceive is necessary to get that much needed attention in their immediate circumstances.

The answer? Pay positive attention to your kids! Help them feel included.

Children need positive, healthy boundaries: Consistent boundaries that expand as they mature through the experience of living their life and making choices.

Why do we put small children in playpens?

To give them boundaries!

A playpen is a physical boundary designed to help that child be safe. The child (and the parent) can be more relaxed when the child is in the playpen because they can see the physical boundaries that they can play in. The child can feel that the parent is more relaxed so they can focus on exploring their own little world without concern for safety.

As the child ages, they outgrow the playpen, but they do not outgrow the need for boundaries.

Would you let your five year old child drive your car? Of course not. This is a boundary!

Would you let your five year old child have free rein in your laptop? Of course not!

However, you would let this child explore his home environment (under your watchful eye) and let him figure out what his world is all about. As the child learns to crawl, and then to walk, the boundaries are expanded to allow for more growth. This process should be an ever expanding process, until such time as this person is a fully mature adult.

Children need to have consciously decided boundaries determined by their parents that support the child's ability to be as safe as possible while exploring their world at the current level they are at.

There may be many people who do not agree with me; but I am going to state it anyway. I believe that children are not equal to their parents when it comes to having the right to make decisions about their lives, or how they choose to express themselves.

I personally believe that rights and privileges are earned. Children do have the right to be treated lovingly, respectfully and to explore their world in an acceptable manner to the parents.

In the process of maturing, children need and want to expand their boundaries and will push to find those boundaries.

Parents need to understand and manage what the parameters of those boundaries are at any given time. They need to be consistent, and they need to be willing to interact maturely with the child to discuss reasons for the boundaries as the child matures.

Although I certainly support children's rights, children are only as mature as their internal development supports. In that, a person who is not fully mature does not have the capacity or faculties to make decisions at the same level as a mature person.

Children should be supported constantly to make decisions; however, their decision needs to be rubber stamped by the parents as a means of protecting the child from unnecessary harm and undesirable learning experiences.

When children are raised to understand and accept the pecking order, they will be happier themselves and the home environment will benefit. NO discounting!

I think if we were to go look at the statistics, wherever they are, regarding children who get into trouble, we will definitely find a parallel between the appropriate setting and maintaining of healthy boundaries and the acting out of the involved children.

Children need to be treated like people. As adults, we need to realize and accept that children do not have the understanding, experience or processing skills that we have. We, therefore, need to communicate with them in a manner that is at their level.

This does not mean talking to them in baby talk. It does mean physically getting yourself down to their level when you talk to them.

I would presume that you might have noticed that most adults are considerably bigger than children. When a much bigger adult goes off the deep end and starts ranting or barking orders, the child becomes afraid and will do whatever it can to protect itself.

Can you imagine what it looks like and feels to a small person when the much larger adult who towers over them (and is supposedly their protector) acts out in a way that is terrifying to them? Of course, they are going to act out! They feel afraid!

When it becomes a regular occurrence, it becomes a part of their belief system. They will automatically react to anything even similar to this learned experience. They feel unsafe!

Another point I wish to make, as well, is about how children communicate.

Young children who are not at the stage of speaking yet, still express themselves. It just is not in the form we are used to communicating in. It is our job to communicate with them in a way they understand. They just want to be heard!

At the back of this booklet I have included some techniques one can use for communicating with small children in a manner that overrides the need for them to speak verbally.

I recall one time walking down the street in a city that was known for its hills. A mom was walking near me with her son who was about 4 years of age, as well as with a toddler who was safely nestled in the stroller. The little boy was a typical little guy who wanted to run about everywhere.

As they were heading down the hilly sidewalk, he kept bolting ahead. Of course, mom was worried about his safety but could not manage him adequately because of the stroller.

She kept yelling at him "Stop" "Stop" "Stop"... but of course he did not.

Everything turned out okay and she finally got him settled down but as I watched this episode I wondered if the little boy even knew what the word "stop" means?

The mom was making a presumption that could have been very costly!

One of my favorite situations happened in front of me involving my friend's son-in-law and his daughter.

The son-in-law is a big guy, about 6 ft 3. His daughter was about 2 ½ years old at the time. We were in a big store shopping when all of a sudden the daughter started screaming and acting out.

Very quickly, the dad got himself right down to the daughter's level, reached his hand gently out for her to grab without touching her, then quietly invited her to come to him.

He just stayed in that position until she finally settled down and reached into him. Once she was feeling safe but still screaming, he asked her what it was she wanted. She kept pointing and screaming.

Again, quietly, he spoke to her and told her that he did not understand her screaming and that if she wanted him to understand she would have to "use her words". He then continued to sit there until she stopped screaming. She then took a deep breath and, in her words, told him her concerns.

Dad then remedied the situation and we all carried on. Eventually, the daughter learned that screaming was not a functional form of communication and chose to use her words instead.

The lesson inside these examples is that children need to understand and know they are safe. Although safety is a natural function of our subconscious mind, it still requires a great deal of persistence in training the children what it really means to be truly safe.

Children need to have and to know consistent boundaries that are applied lovingly, continuously and appropriately for their level of maturity.

For older children, this still holds true, however, a big concern to me in our society today is that older children are often taught to believe that they have the same rights to act and express themselves as the adults do.

I again reiterate that children, no matter their age, only have the rights and privileges they have earned. This sense of entitlement that is the rage in our society today is having catastrophic outcomes and needs to be reined in.

If we continue with this lack of boundaries, our society will continue to degrade, and our economy and society will falter as children are unable and unwilling to participate in a mature, helpful manner that contributes to the wonderful life created for them.

As it is, we are raising a section of society that unjustly feels privileged and not obligated to have considerations for the rules of society and the rights of others.

The only way to prevent this from becoming engrained is to start training children from the earliest years to respect themselves and any others.

Children who are raised in a safe environment do not grow up to be gang members, or dangerous drivers, homeless or parasites on society.

Children raised in safe environments grow up to be healthy, prosperous, engaged individuals who truly embrace and enjoy life and help to foster such feelings in others.

Before we leave the topic of safety and the development of healthy boundaries, I feel that it is important to bridge a conversation regarding a very popular topic of today.

This topic is about parenting itself.

How many people does it take to raise a child in a healthy manner?

We live in a very complicated society where every person seems to believe they have the right to do what they want and do it how they want and that is okay.

This is ego based thinking. Most unfortunately, most of this kind of thinking is just rebellious and does not work for anyone involved.

It takes a man and a woman to create a child. Children are born with the essence of male and female inside them in their creation. Children need to have the influences of both males and females in their lives in order to grow and mature into healthy individuals.

I want to be clear that my intention is not to be condescending toward single parenting or homosexual parenting. My purpose is to point out that because children have both a male and female aspect inside themselves, they need to have both a positive male and a positive female influence over the long term of their maturing process in order to fully know and be their true and complete selves.

A man or a woman, no matter their sexual orientation, cannot provide the essence of the other gender no matter how they try. It just is not in them. Only a woman can provide female essence and only a man can provide the male essence.

Even though, in the grand scheme of our design, we do carry the programming and capacities of both the sexes, our minds are principally oriented by the gender of our body. Even in homosexuals, men and women think and operate differently.

If a child is raised in a single parent environment, for the child to be healthiest, the child needs to have a person of the other gender (and preferably someone in for the long-haul) to balance their needs. The two people do not need to live together but they do need to work together to give this child the best shot at life.

In homosexual relationships, the same needs to be applied as in a single parent relationship.

If we truly wish for our children to have the best chance in succeeding in all levels of life, we need to be open and willing to allow other people to be involved in their upbringing.

Even in heterosexual partnerships with children, the child gains a wider perspective in life if there are more caregivers involved in the raising of that child. Aunts, uncles, older siblings, grandparents and good friends can provide essential support for a child while giving Mom and Dad a well-deserved break. After all, raising children is more than a full time job!

In providing a safe environment for a child, it is essential that the parents create a safe, supportive and comfortable environment for themselves too!

A truly safe environment for children needs to include other people, so they can learn to feel safe to explore the world outside of the environment created by Mom and Dad.

After all, the little bird must fly from the nest one day! Simulating the outside world in a managed and effective way provides the basic structure for the child to manage its role in the outside world.

Chapter 9

The Third Need

We are finally getting down to the nitty gritty of providing for the needs of healthy children!

When adults know themselves and are committed to advancing themselves as human beings and when these people choose to create and raise children in a truly safe environment, the most important aspect of caring for the needs of the children can be made manifest.

The third need for healthy children is:

An environment that provides and encourages their own personal growth through experiences in life.

Whether we choose to believe it or not, we are born into this life to grow in our own individual manner. By design, we are committed to become the most we are capable of becoming as a human being or human spirit. However, life has a way of getting in the way.

By default, all people, no matter their age or circumstance will always do what they need to do in order to feel safe. When children are not provided with a truly safe and respectful environment, they learn to cope. Their need to "feel" safe is either their first priority or their only priority. The fear of not feeling safe is so powerful that it can override all other occurrences. Their coping becomes their mechanism for safety.

It is up to us as parents to be conscious of our own methods of getting through life and ensuring that our offspring develop and express outcomes that serve them in the best possible way.

When children are born, their mind is basically an empty slate. It is up to their parents to develop and implement an ongoing plan to ensure that the children in their charge are provided with the very best opportunities to become the amazing people they already are.

This does not mean having to send them to the best schools and dress them in the best, most fashionable outfits or provide them with every bobble that the big guns say they have to have in order to be truly acceptable to their peers.

It does mean spending plenty of quality time with them, interacting in meaningful ways such as chatting, cooking, teaching them how to do useful things, going for walks in nature, and, most important, helping them to explore their own interests in life.

Every child is born with a special set of interests that are brought forward through their own karma. It is our job as parents and care givers to help each child to work their way through a myriad of adventures while observing, testing and unveiling the story that lies inside this person.

It is our job to help each child to discover and understand who they are. This again falls into the development of boundaries. Boundaries are safe when consistently applied; however, boundaries also need to make sense and should be appropriate to their age.

Children need to understand and accept basic concepts about themselves that help them to define themselves. In this statement, I also reserve the aspect of maintaining a more open set of boundaries that support self-knowledge.

Inside this self –knowledge, there is room to play as part of the exploring.

Now I know I am going to get flack for stating my perspective on this subject, but I do it in respect with a desire for common sense.

Here goes!

There are two aspects to human beings. As I have previously stated, these are the physical and non-physical. The physical aspect is what we can see as well as what we perceive as our methodology for interacting in this world. This includes our physical senses and emotions.

This non-physical aspect I am referring to is the soul.

The soul has no gender. The only purpose of the soul in a living being is to collect information with which it grows and becomes stronger as part of the Cosmic Whole.

The gender of a normal healthy person is determined and validated simply by looking between the infant's legs. Animals of any kind including human beings only come in two genders: male and female.

It is important for children to understand their gender because they will naturally and predominantly express the nature of that gender in their lives. It seems that usually boys like trucks and girls like dolls. However, there is no shame at all in little boys playing with dolls or girls liking to play with trucks after all; being male or female is not an exact science.

As their life progresses, they will gravitate to activities that express their true nature, as long as the parents consciously guide, support and give them supported space along the way.

Providing a safe environment that includes lots of exploratory discussions will help the child to make choices and mold their life according to their inner drives.

As children mature, so must the conversations. When puberty arrives, the discussions and the training need to be ramped up. With the onset of all those hormones that occur during this period, a lot of chaos ensues.

The child in puberty is faced with a lot of unknowns that they need to sort out. Your being there for them with an open, supportive and knowledgeable mind will help them through this time in the best manner possible.

I think one of the biggest mistakes we make in helping our children grow is to rush them into being grown up too fast. This is a social issue. We are inundated with television shows depicting teens acting like adults, when they clearly are not.

With a great deal of love, respect and conversation inside the family setting, these children can get a whole lot better perspective on life from their family life than they can from a television show. The end result will be happier and healthier adults who can then perpetuate the healthy kids program.

The ultimate goal in raising our children is to be mentors for them so they can grow to become all they can be. Creating and maintaining a fluid structure that supports each of the children in their own way helps them to feel safe. When children feel safe, they can more easily focus on exploring their worlds and determining how they want to express their lives.

When children do well with their lives as they progress along, they are easier to live with, do better in school, have better friends and become better grownups.

Inevitably, issues are going to arise from time to time, as life has a way of providing us with unscheduled learning opportunities. Children are going to act in ways that are not acceptable to the parents at times. Welcome to life.

If we remember as we engage in these challenging times, that they are just learning situations and that as we each engage in the situation in a safe, supportive and respectful manner, the situation will be handled so everyone grows, and the situations easily becomes history.

Remember, the only reasons children act out are because they are looking for boundaries or find themselves in situation they do not have enough life experience to handle well.

When they push against a current boundary, it is going to challenge the parents' authority. Handled incorrectly, it magnifies the problem.

Recognize the situation for what it is, handle it correctly through positive interactive engagement and the issue is dealt with. Love them and help them to learn life in a constantly up reaching manner, so they feel loved, challenged and inspired.

Overall growth of a child needs to include recognition and training on all levels of their person. This can be a little tricky if a person is not "religious". Many healthy families understand and work well in providing their children with good training in the physical, mental and emotional realms but tend to fall short in the spiritual realm.

It is not my purpose at this point to direct anyone towards religion. It is my point to point out that religion is only a tool that provides direction toward spirituality.

In respect to all, each person must choose any of the paths that work for them according to their needs and their perception of life. Since this is not a discussion about the pros and cons of religion, I will leave it at that.

Spirituality is a completely separate topic. I feel that it is important to include spirituality in the process of raising children. It is completely up to the parent as to how this will be implemented.

I am going to include my perspective of where and how spirituality can be included as a non-religious activity.

To me, spirituality means connection with all that exists.

Everything that exists is connected to me and I am connected to all else. Therefore when I interact with other people, I choose to come from a place of respect and connection. I choose to care about myself and others as I engage with them.

I am also a part of nature. I am a part of nature as a part of the animal kingdom and choose to engage from this perspective. I embrace all nature and revel in its beauty. I feel responsible for the destruction we are causing on this planet and choose to help to improve our situation.

I feel life, I feel the life force within me. I feel the life force within you. I feel the life force in the world around me.

This is spirituality. If you choose to add on any formalized structure to that, so be it.

Giving, and consciously supporting, the widest berth to your children to allow them to grow in the best way possible to become the best expression they can manifest is our most important job as parents.

Loving and supporting your kids enough to let them be and become themselves in their most fulfilling way is our ultimate goal!

Chapter 10

Summing it up

Love is the one thing we all desire, and yet, it is the one thing we always have.

As human beings, we seem to have been blessed with the ability to hide what we most want in plain sight. After all, love is an innate aspect of who we are, and is the basis of everything that exists.

The challenge I offer to you, after reading this book is for you to find the real love that always has existed in your life.

This may require contemplating what we mean by love. It may also require your investigating how you perceive and integrate love into your life.

We are never without love. We are often without understanding.

It is our job as adult human beings and as parents to discover how we interpret love in our life.

It is through becoming detached from our belief systems that we can gain clarity about how we do our lives and how we give and receive love.

We learned the art of loving through our relationships with our parents and other caregivers. It is our responsibility to ensure that the love we give to our children is what we truly want for ourselves.

By actively loving our children, we set the intention of knowing ourselves and making healthy choices. We do the best to provide a safe environment that grows and expands with each child as they learn how to live in their own lives.

We implement actions in our lives and the lives of our children that assist and support them in the process of coming to know themselves, their world and what they can become as healthy, responsible adults.

It is by helping ourselves to love, it is by teaching our children to be loving beings that the world will heal. By getting beyond our "selves", we can integrate in the energy of love and consciously help to expand it throughout our universe.

It is only through love that we can truly exist and flourish. It is only through true safety that we can ever truly know true love.

Bonus Chapter

Tools for Effective Parenting

Some of the information in this chapter may seem like a reiteration of information we have already discussed; however, these are important points that lead to the most important point in this chapter... developing non-physical tools for managing your relationships.

In this section, we will discuss various aspects that will assist you in helping your child be the amazing child they were born to be. By being a proactive, committed and consciously involved parent, you will get the best reward of all, a happy child!

Psychologists say that over 80% of all communication occurs non-verbally. Use this to your advantage.

The first step in being the best parent possible is to acknowledge that each of you are a shining example of the gender you are. Therefore, your children will model that aspect of themselves through how they interpret what they extract from you.

Have you ever watched a man and his son walking together? The likelihood is they walk the same gait. Why?

The son learned it from watching his dad, so he copied it.

Being aware of this fact should not be scary! If you feel the pressure just increased on your demand to be a great parent, this is a time to recognize your own self-perspective.

Just be yourself! Choose to be relaxed and good with how you express your life. Just be mindful that your children are watching you.

Here is an example of where a parent could have been more mindful:

A dad and his son were out riding their bikes. The son was riding well just following along behind dad... right through a stop sign!

How is dad going to feel when:

a) son gets hit by a car doing the same thing

b) son gets into accidents while driving a car from not following the rules

c) son gets into trouble at school for disobeying rules.

It all boils down to the same thing!

Dad set the example that rules do not apply to him! Son is only copying him!

On the other side- Dad religiously gets up extra early every morning, so he can do his set of exercises and get outside and run 10 miles before work. As son gets old enough, dad encourages son to finally join him after years of casually mentioning how great it feels.

How is this son going to behave?

He loves his dad and follows his example. The likelihood is that this boy will mature into a healthy individual.

Children do have the ability to choose, and they will choose incorrectly. That is part of the process. They need to learn what is right and what is wrong. They also need to learn what works for them as part of exploring their own personal perspective of the world.

Each child will learn some things from the mom and some from the dad and some they will figure out themselves. Welcome to life!

As a parent, it is our duty to observe the child and guide them gently to choose that which is truly best for them. This may mean letting them make many mistakes, but not letting them give up on themselves because it is too hard.

This does not mean forcing them to follow the family traditions! They do not have to take up the career that one of the parents has... unless they show a strong interest and aptitude for it.

When a child shows an unacceptable trait, it is usually one of two things:

a) a cry for attention

b) they are experimenting, trying to do something they do not have a clear concept of.

Your job is to recognize what they are doing and why!

Recognize the emotion attached to the activity. Reading their facial expression and any body language will give you clues. Monitor the situation, discuss it with your spouse and when the appropriate time occurs, guide the child lovingly and patiently to resolve the issue.

Children need boundaries! They crave boundaries and will push to find them. Even in this modern world of allowing children to make their own choices, they want and need their parents to love them enough by showing them boundaries!

You, as parents, need to determine what those boundaries are and to keep them in place, relaxing them only as you see fit, depending on the child's maturity.

If you start right from the birth of the child consciously placing boundaries on the child's actions, the child will become an easier person to interact with. Keeping your child in a playpen to limit their mobility is much better than disciplining the child for getting into mischief.

However, putting enough toys in the playpen to keep them happily busy is a must or they will tell you, in no uncertain terms, they are bored.

By consciously making good decisions regarding boundaries, the child will be more settled and happier thus making your life more pleasant.

Once we have the general atmosphere worked out, the emotional levels will be much easier to manage and live with. This now opens the door to using tools that have not commonly been offered to parents that will assist in keeping things happy, positive, and best for all.

The Non-Physical tools

As was stated earlier, about 80% of all training for the child occurs non-verbally. This leads us to the concept that the true training of a child should largely be focused on non-verbal triggers.

The most important non-verbal key is your own display of emotions. Be real, as life is generally not a perfect expression, but be mindful that ongoing displays of anger, control and other less than preferable actions will be absorbed and reflected in the child.

Everyone wants to feel safe. When a child feels the energy of a less than desirable emotion, whether directed at them or not, their feeling of safety is disrupted.

A safe child is an easy child to live with. When children have an ongoing challenge of feeling safe in what they perceive as an unsafe environment, they are going to be far more difficult to live with.

If you and/or your spouse does not feel safe and commonly expresses emotions that are challenging to the child, it would be best for both of you to get help and access tools that will help you to become more stable expressions.

The exercises posted on my website: www.powerfulyoupowerfulme.com/videos[1] are valuable tools to assist you in managing the activities of your mind. Learning how to release and reframe undesirable beliefs will help you express yourself as a more wholesome and healthier individual and parent.

Other activities such as physical exercise, walks in nature, meditation, playing games with your children and others where a sense of positive energy is expressed will help you and your child feel safer.

If you would like to learn more about your belief systems and how to manage them, please read my book: Embracing The Blend. Our mind works exactly the same way a computer does. This book provides great information about how your personal software works and how you can manage it.

After all, you are born with the ability to manage and make changes in how your mind works. You just need to know you can and then implement the tools to be able to make the changes you desire.

The next non-verbal tool that is essential to managing and nurturing your child is touch.

Human beings love to be touched. The first choice in being touched is always positive touch. The laying of a hand on them gently for no particular reason, messing up their hair just for the fun of it, a big hug are all examples of positive touch.

Positive touch should always be done with no ulterior motives. Children are sensitive to the truth. If an action has a negative intent to it, they will pick it up!

---

1. http://www.montyritchings.com/videos

Scruff up your child's hair or give them a hug just because you wish to express that you love them!

The Psychic Side of Human Communication

There is another side to non-verbal communication which goes on whether we choose to recognize it or not, therefore it is best to recognize it and use it as a positive tool.

That tool is your own psychic ability!

We all have a psychic side. It is just another layer of our ability to communicate information between each other. It does not require taking courses to become a psychic.

If you desire to have more knowledge of your non-physical communications systems, my book: **Chakras Demystified** is a great resource. By understanding the various levels of energetic communication, we all possess and interact through, you will be able to consciously communicate more effectively.

You can use these tools when interacting with any person, including yourself. The goal is always to assist them in feeling more positive and safer. The more positive a person is, the easier they are to get along with.

Here are some tools you can work with to deal with specific situations:

Communicating with babies

Learn to understand what babies are saying when they are verbalizing. Whether it is general chatter or crying, they are attempting to communicate with you. If you listen quietly to the communication they are offering, you will learn to understand what they are trying to tell you. This is particularly true of crying. If you take the time to learn the different sounds of their cries, you will soon pick up what their message is. Believe me, the cry from a dirty diaper is quite different from one of pain or from being hungry!

Communicating with children in distress

If a child is in distress, of course, you will know what they want so you can help them. Sometimes, they are just wanting attention, so here is a technique that you can do from a distance, particularly at night.

Visualize yourself standing near the child, take a series of deep breaths while visualizing rubbing their back in a downward stroke. You can imagine them in a cloud of gold light as well if you like. Very quickly, they will pick up the energy and relax. The downward stroke helps to ground them to the earth. Communication fulfilled without even getting out of bed!

Increasing your intention to connect with another person.

Visualize sending gold light to a person you wish to increase your connection with. (Always with no ulterior motive)

Helping another to deal with a situation without verbally interacting.

Send the same gold light to a person who is struggling with some issue. It is essential that when you send this gold light that you send it with no other intention than to support them in moving through whatever is causing them to need your support. Potentially manipulative thoughts and gold light do not mix!

Sending your child positive thoughts non-verbally to help them grow

Send your child positive messages through your mind to theirs without verbalizing. Keep the messages simple and clear. "I love you unconditionally", "I choose to know and accept the real you", "Let yourself be", "Be safe" are all forms of positive messages you can send to your child. These are especially effective while they are sleeping. You can sit near them on their bed and silently project the thoughts to them.

The most importance aspect of working with you child, or any other person, is to be sincere and honest in your communication.

Know you own desires. Know your own agenda before you attempt to use any of these tools. Be clear!

A child who is constantly raised in an imperfect but positive environment will be an easier person to know and love. It all starts with you!

About The Author

Monty Ritchings specializes in helping people understand what drives them. For over thirty years Monty has been a practicing energetic healing facilitator, core belief counselor, medical intuitive and facilitator of programs that assist people in understanding and empowering their own inner self.

As a proud dad and grandpa, Monty treasures watching his family and the families of friends grow and reveal the beauty and true nature of each of the people involved.

As our world changes and evolves, Monty writes and publishes books and booklets in hopes that the words help to raise the consciousness of the human species.

Monty's website is www.powerfulyoupowerfulme.com[2].

2. http://www.powerfulyoupowerfulme.com

Books by Monty C. Ritchings

Embracing The Blend

Chakras Demystified

Stamp Out Stress

Let's Get Hiking

The Ascenders Return To Grace Books 1 & 2

Monty's Videos are available on the website at www.powerfulyoupowerfulme.com[3]

Conscious Mind Management

Living in Present Time

Quieting The Mind

These videos were recorded to provide you with easy to learn and powerful tools for stress management. The more you can manage your mind, the better a parent you can be!

---

3. http://www.powerfulyoupowerfulme.com

About the Author

Monty has been a student of mysticism for over 40 years. He is a member of the Rosicrucian Order AMORC, the oldest mystical body in the western world, He has also studied and practices arcane arts such as Reiki, Core Belief Engineering, Jin Shin Jyustu and more.

Monty lives in Canada near Vancouver.

Read more at https://montyritchingsbooks.com.